Snow White
and the
Seven Dwarfs

GW00706071

Methuen Children's Books

London

Snow White

Once upon a time a queen pricked her finger as she sat embroidering. Looking at the drops of blood she said, 'I hope I have a daughter with hair black as ebony, skin white as snow, and cheeks rosy as blood.'

Not long after she had a baby daughter. Her hair was black, her cheeks were rosy, and her skin was so fair she was named Snow White.

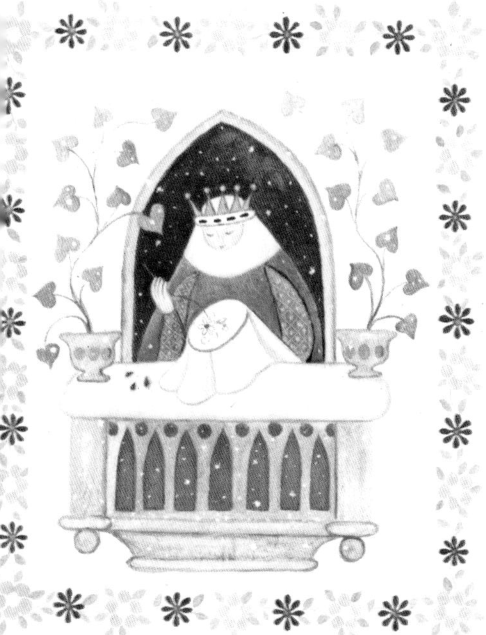

Alas, the queen died, and after a year the king married a new wife. She was so proud and vain that she could not bear to think that anyone was more beautiful than she was. Every day she would ask her mirror:

Mirror, mirror, on the wall,
Who is the fairest one of all?

and the mirror always replied:

You are the fairest one of all.

But Snow White grew up to be so beautiful that one day the mirror answered the queen:

> *Queen, you are very fair,*
> *'tis true,*
> *But Snow White is lovelier*
> *far than you.*

The queen turned pale with rage. She began to hate Snow White. At last her envy became so violent that she sent for a huntsman and told him to take Snow White into the forest and kill her.

In the forest the huntsman told Snow White what the queen had ordered him to do. Sadly he drew out his knife. Snow White shrank back in terror. 'Oh, please, dear huntsman, do not kill me.'

The huntsman put away his knife. 'Poor little princess, I will *say* I have killed you. But you must never go back to the palace.' He left her with a heavy heart. At first Snow White cried and cried. Then, terrified, she ran deeper and deeper into the forest.

It began to get dark, and Snow White, stumbling over tree roots and torn by brambles, was exhausted. And then in a glen she saw a little house – a friendly house. The front door was closed – nobody about. The garden was full of flowers, and on the roof a little bird sang an evening song as if to welcome her.

She knocked on the door – no answer. She tried the latch, lifted it and went in.

Everything in the house was small and clean and pretty. On the round table was a white cloth, and on that were seven little bowls and spoons. Snow White was very hungry, so she took a sip from the first bowl, then from the second, and so on all round the table, while mice watched her with interest.

She felt very tired now, so she climbed the stairs to look for somewhere to sleep.

Upstairs were seven little beds in a row. Snow White lifted the cover off the first one, lay down, and went fast asleep. When the owners of the house, seven dwarfs, came home, they were puzzled to find that someone had eaten a little from each of their bowls. But they blamed the mice. After their supper they climbed the stairs to bed.

What a surprise! There lay Snow White. They marvelled at her beauty, but did not wake her.

When Snow White woke in the morning and saw the seven dwarfs she was very frightened. But she soon found how kind they were. She told them all about her wicked stepmother. 'You must stay with us,' they said. 'But let no one into the house, for if your stepmother finds you are still alive she will do you harm.'

So Snow White stayed with them. After the dwarfs had left each morning to dig for gold in the mountain, she scrubbed and polished the house, and cooked a meal ready for them at night.

But the queen's mirror told her:

Queen, yours is indeed a beauty rare,
But Snow White living in the glen
With the seven little men,
Is a thousand times more fair.

The queen was furious. So the huntsman had *not* killed Snow White! She disguised herself as an old woman selling pretty laces and ribbons, and went to the little house in the glen. 'Here's a fine silken cord to lace up your dress,' she said. She pulled the cord so tightly that Snow White fell down as if dead. And so the dwarfs found her. They cut the cord, and Snow White breathed again.

Once more the queen went to her mirror only to find that Snow White still lived. She tried to trick her with a poisoned comb. When that failed she disguised herself again and offered a sweet juicy apple to Snow White. 'See, I'll take a bite from the green side,' she said. 'Taste how delicious the red side is!'

Snow White thought there could be no harm in an apple. She bit into it – and now she seemed dead indeed. Nothing the dwarfs did could make her come back to life.

This time when the queen asked her mirror the question it answered:

You are the fairest now of all.

And the queen was satisfied.

In the little house in the glen the dwarfs sat round Snow White's body for three days and wept. How could they live without their dear Snow White? She looked so beautiful that they made a glass coffin to keep her in. They carried it up the mountain and heaped flowers round it. The birds and the animals came to mourn poor Snow White.

One day a prince rode by and saw Snow White in the glass coffin. Instantly he fell in love. 'Let me take the coffin to my castle,' he begged, 'so that I may at least look on her face all day.'

The dwarfs refused, but being kind-hearted at last they agreed. Gently they lifted the coffin, but one of them stumbled. The poisoned apple flew out of Snow White's mouth. She opened her eyes. Quickly the dwarfs removed the glass lid and Snow White sat up. She saw the prince kneeling beside her, and fell in love with him at once.

Snow White said a loving farewell to the dwarfs. Then the prince lifted her onto his horse, and they rode off to they castle where they lived happily ever after.

As for the wicked stepmother, when she asked her mirror the question it answered:

O Queen, you are of beauty rare,
But Snow White the bride
is far more fair.

The Queen screamed, turned purple with rage, and fell dead. And that was the end of *her*.

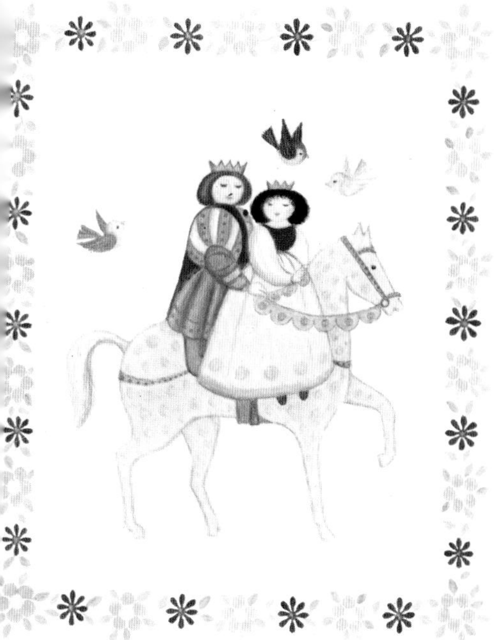

British Library Cataloguing in Publication Data

Jones, Olive
    A little box of fairy tales.
    1. Tales
    I. Title II. Crespi, Francesca
    398.2′1   PZ8.1

ISBN 0-416-24690-7

First published in Great Britain in 1982 by
Methuen Children's Books Ltd.,
11 New Fetter Lane, London, EC4P 4EE.
Illustrations copyright © 1982 by Francesca Crespi.
Text copyright © 1982 by Methuen Children's Books Lt

Printed in Singapore by
Tien Wah Press (Pte) Ltd.